Published by Sweet Cherry Publishing Limited
Unit 36, Vulcan House,
Vulcan Road,
Leicester, LE5 3EF
United Kingdom

First published in the US in 2022
2022 edition

2 4 6 8 10 9 7 5 3 1

ISBN: 978-1-80263-050-3

Soccer Rising Stars: Trent Alexander-Arnold

Cover design and illustrations
by Sophie Jones

Lexile® code numerical measure L = Lexile® 990L

www.sweetcherrypublishing.com

Printed and bound in Turkey

SOCCER RISING STARS

TRENT ALEXANDER-ARNOLD

THE UNOFFICIAL STORY

Written by
HARRY MEREDITH

Sweet Cherry

CONTENTS

1

A SCOUSE FAIRY TALE

Roaring Liverpool fans belted out the words to "You'll Never Walk Alone"— a famous song that, when sung by tens of thousands of people at the same time, sends goosebumps down the arms of any *scouser*—a person from Liverpool.

The Liverpool team lined up to shake the opposition's hands. Trent Alexander-Arnold, like his teammates, wore a dark-red jacket to keep warm on this cool spring evening. Beneath it, he was wearing the home gear of the team he had supported since childhood. Today, he was representing Liverpool in a crucial Champions League tie.

It was the second leg of the semifinal against Barcelona. The first leg in Spain had not gone to plan. Inspired by Lionel Messi, the Argentinian wonder and to many

the greatest soccer player of all time, Barcelona had sent their fans home smiling after a convincing 3-0 win. Even the most devoted Liverpool supporters found it hard to make a case for their team's route to victory. Not only were they going to have to score four goals to win, or at least one more goal on aggregate than Barcelona, there was an additional hurdle that they needed to clear. Liverpool were playing without two of their star players: Roberto Firmino and Mohamed Salah. Both players unfortunately missed the match due

to injuries. But despite all of the pre-match hopelessness, there was still ninety minutes of soccer to play. And in front of a roaring Anfield crowd, in a stadium known for its intense atmosphere, there was always a chance.

The Reds could hardly have wished for a better start. Only seven minutes into the match, Jordan Henderson wriggled through the Barcelona defense and delivered a strike that stung the gloves of the goalkeeper, Marc-André ter Stegen. He was unable to hold on to the ball and it

bounced to the feet of Divock Origi—
a player who had found game time
hard to come by during his stint
at Liverpool. His path to the first
team had often been blocked by the
amazing performances of the club's
superstars. But now, while Firmino
and Salah were injured, he had a
chance—and he was going to take it.
As the ball bounced to Origi, he

coolly passed it into the
net and Anfield erupted.
Instead of celebrating,
Origi raced to the
halfway line.

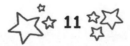

The game was on.

In the 14th minute, Barcelona showed Liverpool that they remained a threat. Left back Jordi Alba bolted into the Liverpool penalty area and sent the ball back to his captain, Messi. Messi struck the ball at the Liverpool goal, and it was only just tipped over the bar by a stretching Alisson. Liverpool may have scored first, but Barcelona wanted to remind them of their overall advantage. The Spanish side was still leading 3-1 on aggregate—the total score counted from the first and second legs of a soccer match.

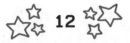

Only a few minutes later, Barcelona charged again. This time the ball found its way to the feet of Philippe Coutinho, a former Liverpool player and fan favorite during his time at the club. But on that night, he received no love from his former fans. Coutinho struck the ball and Alisson dived to the ground, palming it away from goal. It was beginning to look like an away team goal was coming.

The first half ebbed and flowed with attacks from both teams. The referee called a halt to the first half, and Liverpool headed into the locker room needing a miraculous second half performance. Jürgen Klopp, the popular Liverpool manager, led a halftime team talk.

"I want you to give me everything you've got," said Klopp, as he sat down with his players. Trent, sitting on a bench, placed his sports drink on the ground and leaned forward. "We are without two of the best attackers in world soccer." Klopp continued. "The whole world thinks this is impossible. But this is Liverpool Football Club. Think back to our Champions League comeback in

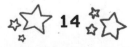

2005. There's a reason why this club has won this tournament five times. Can you hear those fans roaring in the Kop? Do it for them. Do it to silence the critics who say we can't. Do it because we're Liverpool!"

The team went into the second half pumped. Klopp made a substitution and brought on the Netherlands midfielder Georginio Wijnaldum.

It was time to give everything.

In the 53rd minute, Sadio Mané played a cross-field ball to Trent. He tried to head it to a teammate, but the header was poor and the ball fell to

the away team. Angered by his mistake, Trent galloped at the Barcelona defender and stole the ball back. He pushed it far in front of him and ran down the right wing before sweeping a cross into the box. Wijnaldum met the cross and side-footed it toward the goal. It scrambled through the arms of the goalkeeper and Liverpool pulled another goal back. The score was now 3-2 on aggregate.

Three minutes later, the small but tricky winger Xherdan Shaqiri, who like Origi had found game

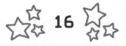

time hard to come by, swung the ball into the box. Wijnaldum leapt above the Barcelona defenders, who were much taller than him, and sent the Liverpool fans into rapture by heading in another goal. The teams were now level. There was no longer just a faint hope of getting a draw out of the game. There was a real possibility that Liverpool could win.

The game settled for a short time. Then with ten minutes remaining, Liverpool earned a corner and Trent placed the ball down. However, before the match he had agreed

with Shaqiri that they would share corner duties, and it was now the Swiss forward's turn. Trent walked away from the ball, but out of the corner of his eye he could see that the Barcelona defense weren't paying attention. He turned around, smashed the ball into the box, and etched his name and this night into Liverpool legend. The ball was met by a thunderous finish by Origi. Liverpool were now ahead.

The entire team sprinted toward the corner, cheering with Trent and Origi. The young right back had just performed an act of soccer brilliance, and his teammates praised him for it. They knew that while Origi was the name on the scoresheet, this crucial goal had come because of Trent's quick-thinking. The team held on to the lead to win the match against all odds.

When Trent Alexander-Arnold took that corner and helped his team to victory he was only 20 years old. He had played a part in a miraculous win for his hometown club. A club that he had supported since he could first kick a ball. This moment went

beyond any young soccer dreams. This was a standard that created endless inspiration for soccer kids across the world.

2

THE KID
FROM WEST
DERBY

Trent Alexander-Arnold was born
on the 7th October 1998, the middle
child to parents Diane and Michael.
His older brother, Tyler, was four
years older, while his younger brother,

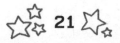

Marcel, arrived three years after him.

Family always meant a lot to Trent. His mother was a driving force behind his development and an incredible source of support. Trent's father was just as important, but in a different manner. He taught Trent to focus on school and helped him plan for his career in soccer. Having two brothers also encouraged Trent to have a competitive edge. They had plenty of opportunities to play soccer at the park. Trent was always the best at soccer, but his brothers had other strengths that they could hold over him. Tyler always won when playing video games, and Marcel often won games such as chess.

One day, a 6-year-old Trent and 10-year-old Tyler were going to play soccer on the field not far from their home, but first they had another plan. With it being school break, they could visit the Melwood training center, a few minutes' walk from their home in West Derby.

The pair of them walked up a steep hill of grass and found themselves next to the training ground border. Surrounded by gates, it was hard to

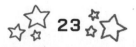

get a good view. But they could hear the thuds of soccer balls being kicked and shouts from players.

"Can I go on your shoulders?" said Trent.

"Okay, but tell me what you see," said Tyler. Trent hopped onto Tyler's back and tried to stretch his neck as far as he could, but he still couldn't quite see. To the side of him there was a crack in the fence.

"Step to the right," said Trent.

Tyler moved, trying not to slip on the grass.

"Stop!"

 Trent brought his eye close to the crack and saw inside Melwood.

"They're all wearing bibs," said Trent. "Yellow against orange. John Arne Riise is in orange and he has the ball. He's just run past Jamie Carragher and ... wait a minute. There's Steven Gerrard!"

Trent was able to catch a glimpse of his soccer icon before his brother lost his balance and the pair tumbled to the ground. They rolled down the hill and were covered in grass stains from head to toe.

Neither of them was hurt and both were on the ground laughing.

"Can't believe Stevie G"s just on the other side!" said Marcel.

Living only a short distance from the Liverpool training ground provided lots of inspiration for the young Trent. Whenever he could he'd visit, whether that was with his brothers, his friends or on his own. He took any chance he could get for a sneak peek at his favorite team.

As well as playing soccer with his brothers and friends, Trent played for local teams on weekends. One

school day, at the age of 6, one of Trent's teachers mentioned an opportunity that would change the young boy's future.

Liverpool FC were holding a community summer camp, and kids from the school were being given a chance to go and play in front of Liverpool scouts.

"So who in the class would like to take part?" asked the teacher. Every boy's hand shot in the air like an

 arrow springing from a bow. Trent had to contain his excitement and stop

himself from leaping up from his chair. However, there was only a set number of spots available and so the teacher had to pick names out of a hat.

As the teacher mixed a  set of names in a hat, Trent crossed his fingers and watched their every move. The first name was called and it wasn't his. The second name was called and it wasn't his either. Then the third name was called ...

"Trent Alexander-Arnold."

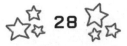

Yes! Now Trent did jump up from his chair. Trent was going to play in the Liverpool FC community summer camp, in front of the team's youth scouts and coaches.

3
LIVERPOOL ACADEMY

A couple of weeks later, Trent was driven to the session by his parents.

"We'd like to sign in, please," said Trent's mom.

The receptionist pressed a few keys on the computer. He peered over the desk. "And who are we signing in?"

he said, smiling at Trent.

"My name's Trent," he said. His mum gave him a nudge. "Oh, and my last name is Alexander-Arnold."

Trent was led to the changing room where there were hundreds of eager young children dreaming of playing for Liverpool.

Once Trent was geared up and ready for the session, his mom crouched and placed her hand on his shoulder.

"There's no pressure," she said. "Just show them how good you are and enjoy yourself. Okay?"

Trent nodded and ran off toward

the coaches, beaming from ear-to-ear. Even on a field filled with children, Trent immediately stood out to the scouts and coaches. He had incredible natural talents and could turn and control the ball with ease. He could also run endlessly, and his determination and enthusiasm shone through the crowded field.

Around fifteen minutes into the training session, as Trent was taking part in soccer drills, one of the scouts went over to his mother.

"Your boy's good," said the scout. "How would you feel about bringing

him here a couple of days a week from now on? We'd really like Trent to come and play for us at the academy."

Not long after that, Trent began spending hours on the Liverpool training field instead of kicking a ball around a field with his brothers. He trained with the academy multiple times a week. He also played two games on a Saturday followed by another game on a Sunday, then did even more training.

All of this soccer was exciting and an incredible opportunity for Trent. But his family had to make a lot of

sacrifices during this time. His older brother often had to miss his own soccer matches because Trent was playing at the academy and their mother couldn't take them both. With Trent's father working away in London, his mother had to free up time to take Trent to training. She also had two other sons to look after. It was the sacrifices made by his parents and his hard work that led to Trent's success within the academy.

As Trent progressed through the club's ranks, they asked him if he could play during the week. This meant that he needed to take some half-days at school. His school said no to this, so Trent moved to Rainhill High School—a school that had partnered with Liverpool FC and agreed to a blend of soccer training and schoolwork.

The move wasn't easy, as the new school was a two-hour journey away from Trent's home. But with the help of his family, and with a large serving of determination, Trent was able to

 thrive in this pressured environment. His busy schedule meant that

he hardly had any time to enjoy the social aspects of teenage life. But that didn't matter. Trent was going to do everything he could to make it as a professional soccer player for Liverpool.

This effort eventually paid off. Trent went on to captain both the under 16 and 18 sides in Liverpool's academy. He was a talented player with an unbreakable commitment to the club. He led by example and inspired those around him to play to the best of their abilities. During his time at the academy, his childhood idol Steven Gerrard said that Trent was going to be a special player in the club's future. Trent could hardly believe it. Not only had his soccer icon noticed him, but he had picked him out as a future talent for the club they both adored.

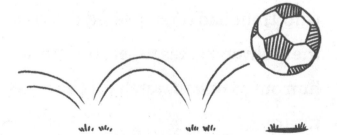

4
THE BALL BOY

Hearing such kind words from a club icon and national soccer hero meant the world to Trent. Steven Gerrard, who Trent had often peered through the Melwood gates to see, had picked him out as one to watch for the future.

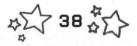

The former club captain saw a lot of himself in Trent—a local scouser growing up not too far away from Anfield with dreams of playing in red. Just as Gerrard had grown up playing on the Merseyside fields dreaming of being John Barnes or Steve McMahon, so Trent had grown up playing on the same turf pretending to be his idol.

When Gerrard led Liverpool to an incredible Champions League comeback in 2005, Trent had watched with all of his friends and family in amazement as a miracle unfolded

 on live TV. At halftime, the Italian side AC Milan held a 3-0 lead and Liverpool were seemingly out of the tie. But led by their captain, Liverpool rallied and were able to bring the game level to 3-3 against all odds. In one of the most exciting Champions League matches of all time, Liverpool won in a nail-biting penalty shoot-out.

But while Trent had been able to revel in Gerrard's career highlights, he also had to go through the lows too. While the club claimed success in the Champions League, it had been a long time since they had achieved success in the Premier League. That was until 2014 when Liverpool, then managed by Brendan Rodgers, had a chance to win the Premier League for the first time in what felt like forever. As an academy player, Trent often got the chance to visit Anfield as a ball boy. And for a crucial home tie in the race for the title against Chelsea, Trent was going to have a front row seat. He'd be closer to the action than any other fan.

Trent was sitting in front of the billboard on a plastic chair. His feet were firmly planted on the ground, his elbows resting on his knees and his eyes locked on the action in front of him. It was coming to the end of the first half and the game was level. Both Chelsea and Liverpool had enjoyed moments of success but had failed to break the deadlock.

Moments before the referee considered blowing the whistle, the ball was played back to Gerrard in between the center-backs. The pass caught Gerrard off guard, and as he panicked he lost his footing and slipped. The opportunistic Chelsea striker Demba Ba stole the ball and ran toward the goal, while the desperate Gerrard chased with every ounce of energy he had. But it was no use. Trent looked on in horror: as did every fan inside the stadium. In an instant, the dreams and hopes of a Premier League triumph were replaced with a cold, numb emptiness.

As the whistle blew for halftime, no one could understand what had just happened. The ball had slipped past Gerrard along with the game, and Chelsea went on to win the match 0-2. It was the pivotal moment in the campaign that started the team's downfall and, in the end, it prevented them from claiming their first Premier League title win in decades. It was Gerrard's best chance at winning the Premier League with his hometown club. But despite his heroics for the club in his seventeen seasons at Anfield, that prize was never won.

This failure created a burning desire in all who followed Liverpool, and it was one that ran deep within Trent. All Liverpool fans craved a Premier League triumph more than anything, and if Trent got the opportunity to play for his team, he was going to do everything he could to end their painful wait.

Over the next couple of years after this heartbreaking loss, Trent's life at the academy changed. Motivated by desire, frustration and hope, Trent worked on his game. It was in central midfield, like Gerrard, where Trent played a lot of his academy soccer. He had the technical ability and strategic vision to excel in midfield, but he also had many traits that suited a modern right back. His athletic ability was an

ideal attribute for a right back that is required to run up and down the field throughout a game. His vision to send long cross-field balls could also be used to find attackers in space.

During this time, the right back role was starting to become a much more attractive position for young soccer players. When Trent was still a child, the position had been seen as a defensive role. In the modern game, though, right backs were becoming an integral part of a team's attack. Trent had the ideal attributes needed for a modern right back.

Therefore, when playing for the U18s, Trent and his coaches agreed that a positional shuffle would be good for Trent and Liverpool. It was a move to increase Trent's chances of breaking into the first team squad.

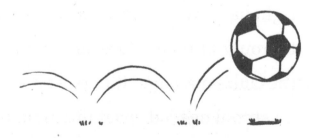

REALIZING A CHILDHOOD DREAM

The move from central midfield to right back worked in Trent's favor. It brought him to the attention of the club's manager, Klopp. And as Liverpool needed cover in the right back position, it fast-tracked Trent's progress with the team.

Then, after years of hard work and sacrifice, it was time. Trent had been selected to play in his first professional soccer game.

His debut took place in the prestigious EFL Cup: an English domestic trophy that, as of 2021, has been won by Liverpool eight times. That's more than any other club in English soccer.

The match was held at Anfield on the 25th October 2016. Instead of standing on the field with a few

hundred spectators, Trent stood in front of a max-capacity crowd with the fans cheering and excited for the match. Despite the new surroundings, Trent was wearing a number that he had carried with him throughout his time at the academy. On the back of his shirt was the number 66: a number given to him when he first joined the club. The academy staff at Liverpool liked to give their young talent high numbers so that they didn't think they'd made it right away when they got their gear. To remember his time at the academy,

Trent held on to the unusual number.

As the players emerged from the tunnel, they shook hands with the opposition and ran onto their side of the field. Trent was in the right back position. He looked from the first row of spectators to the back. He gazed across the stands and saw thousands of Liverpool fans, just like him, excited and hoping for a cup match to remember.

But this was Trent's senior professional debut, so he had to put his wonder to one side. There was no time to appreciate the occasion.

That would come after the game. The focus now was to get into the zone, and put on the best performance he could to help his hometown team progress to the next round of the cup.

Liverpool grabbed the lead within the first ten minutes. Trent was a constant and energetic threat. The young defender flew up and down the wing—not just running for the sake of it, but for strategic plays that led to positive outcomes. It was in the 9th

 minute that one of Trent's dazzling runs applied pressure to a Tottenham player near their own eighteen-yard box. This pressure caused the player to fall to the ground, and Trent's teammate Marko Grujić was able to nick the ball and feed it to Daniel Sturridge. The striker dinked the ball over the onrushing goalkeeper. As the ball went into the net, Trent jumped and punched the air as if he'd scored the goal himself. His delight had taken over as his inner Liverpool fan leapt out. This time instead of jumping up and down in the terraces, he was leaping into the air on the Anfield turf.

In the 64th minute, Sturridge found the net once more and increased Liverpool's lead to two goals. Before the end of the match, Tottenham secured a consolation prize in the form of a 76th minute penalty. It was coolly tucked away by the Netherlands striker Vincent Janssen. However, Liverpool and Trent stood strong, and the youngster helped his team progress to the next round of the cup.

Trent's impressive performance and step up to first-team soccer was noticed by Klopp. Trent would now have many opportunities to showcase his talents to the manager.

During the 2017/2018 season, Klopp rewarded Trent with nineteen appearances in the Premier League. Trent scored once at home against Swansea and produced two assists during the season. It was clear that Trent was a talented player. Before he had even hit the age of 20, he was starting to cement a position in the first team.

6
HEARTBREAK IN KYIV

Despite a mediocre campaign in the Premier League during the 2017/2018 season, Liverpool had performed well in the Champions League—progressing all the way to the final in Kyiv, Ukraine. They had overcome top European teams such as FC Porto,

Manchester City and Roma on their road to the final.

Trent's emergence in the team came with perfect timing. He may have only made nineteen Premier League appearances in that season, but he also played in important Champions League matches. He played his part in the competition and found his name on the team sheet for the Champions League final.

The competition held a special place in Trent's heart because the first game he had gone to watch at Anfield had been a Champions League tie.

Aged seven, Trent went with his family to watch Liverpool play against the Italian giants—Juventus. Thanks to a goal from Luis García, Liverpool won the match 2-1, and Trent's first match as a fan ended in victory. But this time he was not in the stands, shouting and sitting on the edge of his seat. This time *he* was on the field, and he had the chance to make a difference.

The players emerged from the tunnel into a stadium overflowing with proud fans dreaming of victory. A thick mist surrounded the stadium.

Liverpool fans held up their red flags and sang as loudly as they could. The Spanish opposition, Real Madrid, had fans jumping across the stadium in white. The sound of beating drums and Spanish songs clashed with the shouting scousers.

Real Madrid, managed by the famous Frenchman Zinedine Zidane, had won the Champions League two years in a row and were aiming for a treble. Liverpool, historically the most successful English club in the competition, wanted to spoil Real Madrid's hopes and claim the title

for themselves. An atmosphere of excitement, tension and anticipation was in full swing.

In the 15th minute, the ball was lobbed to Cristiano Ronaldo on the right wing. He plucked the ball out of the air with ease and darted at the Liverpool defense. He wriggled his way into the penalty box before being confronted by the towering Virgil van Dijk. With no space left to run, Ronaldo pulled his right leg back and unleashed a shot like releasing a coiled spring. The ball flew over the top of the crossbar, and the Liverpool fans let out a sigh of relief.

Ten minutes later, the ball bounced into Real Madrid's half. Sergio Ramos and Mohamed Salah wrestled for the ball. Salah tried to escape the Spaniard's grip, but Ramos locked his arm under Salah's and the Egyptian was unable to escape. As he tried to pull away his arm was caught, and Salah fell to the ground with Ramos falling on top of him. Because of this, Salah injured his shoulder. He tried to continue, but it was no use. He had to be

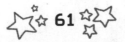

substituted. Liverpool's best player was leaving the field before thirty minutes of the game had even been played. The winger left in tears and was comforted by his teammates. He had made it all the way to his first Champions League final only to have it cruelly taken away from him by an accident.

Almost every Liverpool fan held their head in their hands in dismay. Defeating a team with Real Madrid's quality was already going to be tough. But beating them without one of their star players seemed impossible. Little

did the onlookers know that it was going to become even worse.

In the 51st minute the Liverpool goalkeeper, Loris Karius, tried to throw the ball out of the box to a teammate. But instead, he flung the ball to the feet of the Real Madrid striker standing right in front of him, and the ball cannoned into the net. Those watching the match could hardly believe what had happened. It was a mistake that would dominate

the newspaper headlines for a regular game, let alone a Champions League final.

Five minutes later, Mané lifted
the spirits of the Liverpool hopefuls
with an unexpected equalizer, but
in the end his efforts were in vain.
Not long after, Gareth Bale scored
an incredible overhead kick to send
the Spanish fans into delirium. Bale
scored another goal in the 83rd
minute via a long-distance strike. It
was an attempt that should not have
caused the Liverpool goalkeeper any
problems, but with the terrible error
earlier in the game playing on his
mind, Karius let the shot slip through
his fingers.

At the end of the game, Trent walked onto the podium and collected his runners-up medal. He stood with the rest of his teammates and looked on as the Real Madrid captain, Ramos, lifted the trophy above his head and wildly celebrated with his teammates. It had gone from one of the best nights in Trent's life to one of the worst. He did not want to experience this feeling ever again.

7
WORLD CUP
2018

While Trent's time in Kyiv hadn't
gone to plan there was still a
significant tournament for him
to look forward to. Before the
Champions League final, Liverpool
headed to Marbella for some warm
weather training. This helped to get

the team fit, motivated and ready
to perform in a new environment.
However, the day of the flight
clashed with a rather important
announcement.

The England World Cup 2018 squad
was to be announced.

Trent was yet to play for the
England senior side but had played
for the national youth teams
from the age of 15. Thanks to his
impressive performances there
was a chance that he was going to
be included in the squad. But the
clock was quickly ticking toward the

67

announcement deadline, and Trent had not heard anything.

The Liverpool squad had checked in their suitcases, gone through airport security and were sitting on the shuttle bus taking them to the plane. Trent sat by his friend and teammate Ben Woodburn. He was trying to act calm, but he had his phone on his lap in anticipation. Every other minute, he glanced at the screen waiting for a notification or a call. But each time there was nothing new. Rumors about players who would not be included in the lineup were starting to spread across social media, and from trustworthy sources too. Trent had not seen his name mentioned or heard anything negative. He would likely be up in the clouds when the announcement was made. Surely, if he had been chosen, he would know by now?

Ben nudged Trent. "Stop staring," he said. "They'll call."

Trent nudged his friend back. "I'm not staring," he said. Trent placed his phone in his pocket and looked out of the shuttle window. It was a dream to play for England, and an

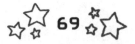

even bigger dream to play for them in a World Cup. But maybe he had been too hopeful. He was yet to play for the squad, and perhaps the manager would only pick players who had trained with the international squad before. A million and one thoughts raced through Trent's mind as he stared at the tarmac outside, covered in a dense morning fog.

Klopp wandered over to Trent. "When's the announcement?" he asked.

"I'm not too sure," said Trent, trying to play it cool.

"Have you heard anything?" asked the Liverpool manager.

"No, I haven't," said Trent, his head drooping.

"Any vacations planned for when the World Cup is on?" asked Klopp.

"No,"said Trent. "I kept it free just in case."

Klopp's lips drew into a smile and a laugh escaped. "Well that's a good thing, then," he said. The entire team turned in their chairs and looked at

 their manager. "Because I've just been on the phone with Gareth Southgate,

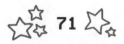

and he wants me to tell you that you're in the squad."

Trent smiled from ear to ear. Everyone around him congratulated him. As the plane took off into the sky, Trent leaned back in his chair staring out of the window, overwhelmed with gratitude. He'd been chosen to play for England in the World Cup!

Before the World Cup in Russia, Trent got the chance to make his England debut at home in front of a max-capacity crowd at Elland Road—the home of Leeds United. Trent played for over two thirds of the match and helped his team to a 2-0 win. This set the team and himself up with the confidence that they could do something special that year.

The team arrived at their hotel in St. Petersburg for the World Cup with a police escort and were greeted by paparazzi. Trent hopped off the coach in his brand-new England training gear and made his way into the hotel. As he admired the building's beauty, it all started to settle in. In summers past, Trent would stay home watching his country play in international tournaments—with

all the celebrations and heartbreaks they involved. He wasn't going to be watching through a TV this time. This year he would be the one on the screen.

During the tournament, Trent only got to play in a single match—a defeat against a talented Belgium side in the group stages. However, despite not getting many minutes on the field, Trent played his part behind the scenes providing competition for the other right backs in the squad. England progressed from their group and made it to the knockout rounds.

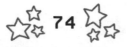

Back in England, there was an incredible feeling that something special could happen with this squad. That the trophy might once again be coming home. Usually, when England played in tournaments, there was a visible nervousness hovering over the players. The pressures and hopes of an entire country weighed on their shoulders. But  during this tournament, a positive and upbeat environment had been created. When Trent wasn't training, he was

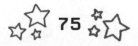

relaxing with the other players in the hotel swimming pool. He would float around on an inflatable unicorn with Harry Maguire as other teammates dived into the pool. There was no unbearable pressure within this team, only a shared desire to make the most of the experience.

This positive outlook made its way onto the field. England progressed in the round of 16 via a penalty shoot-out win against Colombia. England had never before won a penalty shoot-out in a World Cup. In fact, the word "penalties" would bring dread

and traumatic flashbacks to any England fan. But this time the players were victorious, causing millions of fans to jump up in joy, throwing their drinks in the air and celebrating in the streets with relief.

England's journey did not stop there. They defeated Sweden in the quarterfinals 2-0 and made their way for the first time in what felt like forever to the semifinals of a major tournament. The match started well, with England scoring via a Kieran Tripper free kick that sent fans into a frenzy. However, Croatia fought

back, and Trent had to watch from the bench as the Croatians crushed English hopes of a World Cup final and instead took the place for themselves. Despite not winning the tournament, England returned home as heroes—each and every player a proud representative of their club.

Trent hoped that he would have the opportunity to play for England again.

 Instead of watching someone else celebrate, he dreamed of holding the World Cup trophy in his own two hands.

THE BEST
RIGHT BACK?

Out of the famous World Cup
campaign emerged a new Liverpool
hero. Trent may not have brought the
international trophy home with him,
but he was now a member of one of
the most successful England teams

in decades. His newfound glory did not stop his focus. From the first kick of the 2018/2019 Premier League campaign, Trent was as engaged, determined and hungry as ever.

Trent had grown from a local prodigy to one of the Premier League's best right backs. In fact to some observers, he was quickly becoming one of the best right backs in the entire world.

Trent played his part in an incredibly strong Liverpool team that ended up finishing in second place to

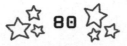

Manchester City, losing the title by a single point.

Liverpool were playing their best soccer in years, and despite their failure to win the title, it was clear that this was a team with the potential to win trophies. Trent finished the year as the third highest assist provider in the entire league. He was only behind the tricky Ryan Fraser of Bournemouth, and Belgian playmaker Kevin De Bruyne. This made Trent the highest assisting defender, providing twelve assists and scoring one goal.

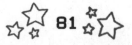

Although Liverpool were unable to win the domestic league, they swiftly put their efforts into doing one better than their previous Champions League campaign. They progressed from the group stages and made their way into the knockout rounds of the tournament. They won against an impressive Bayern Munich team in the round of 16, and then defeated Porto with ease in the quarterfinal. It was there, in the semifinal, where Trent and his teammates pulled off the shock victory against Barcelona—rallying

from a 3-0 first leg defeat to beat the odds in a 4-0 victory at Anfield. But Liverpool were not the only team in the final who had enjoyed an extraordinary route to get there.

Against all odds, fellow Premier League side Tottenham Hotspur stood in the way of Liverpool's Champions League hopes. They had made their way to the final via miraculous wins against Manchester City and Ajax.

One thing was now certain: the Champions League trophy *would* be returning to England. But to which club was still unknown. Would it be

sitting in Tottenham's trophy cabinet? Or would Trent and his teammates shake off their demons from the previous year and bring the trophy back to Anfield?

9

CHAMPIONS LEAGUE REDEMPTION

At the Wanda Metropolitano, home of Atlético Madrid, there was a sea of white and red banners waving in the air. On one side were Tottenham Hotspur fans, hoping to claim their

first ever Champions League trophy. On the other side were Liverpool supporters, excited and hoping to banish the miserable memory of the previous year.

Trent and his teammates lined up with their hands behind their backs as the Champions League anthem boomed across the stadium. Trent was standing proudly. The look in his eyes was not one of boyhood wonder or excitement. It was a look of pure determination.

The Reds kicked off in the fading Spanish sun. The ball was passed

back to van Dijk, and he played a long ball into the opposition half. What followed was a series of aggressive headers, challenges and attempts to win the ball from both sides. It was clear just how much this meant to the players. Henderson played a quick-thinking ball over the Tottenham defense, and Mané ran through on goal. He attempted to make a pass, but the ball struck the arm of the defender Davinson Sánchez. Before twenty-five seconds had been played, everyone in the stadium looked to the referee.

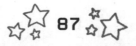

He brought his whistle to his mouth and pointed to the spot.

It was a penalty!

Mohamed Salah, the player so cruelly injured in the previous final, took the ball in his hands and prepared to take the penalty. Ignoring a wave of boos, whistles and shouts, he ran up to the ball and smashed it above the flailing arms of Hugo Lloris. *Goal!* Liverpool had the lead, and the fans let out an enormous roar. But they knew that they could not get too excited. There were many minutes still to play.

In the 17th minute, the ball was played out wide to Trent. He took the ball in his stride and let out a thunderous strike. The ball flew across the goal and had the Tottenham goalkeeper diving to the ground, but it missed the target. Trent sprinted back into position.

In the final few seconds of the first half, Tottenham's Son Heung-min wriggled through the Liverpool defense and played the ball to the

 left. Dele Alli cushioned the ball to Christian Eriksen, but his shot

blazed over the crossbar. The whistle blew for the end of the first half. The Liverpool supporters cheered. It seemed to be their game for the taking. But Liverpool fans know better than any that nothing is ever certain in soccer.

The second half followed the same pattern as the first. Liverpool dominated the play, but they could  not find a second goal. They were only ahead by one, and a single mistake could cost them everything

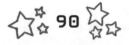

they had worked so hard to build.
Liverpool still held this one-goal lead
as the timer struck the 86th minute.
Liverpool and Trent were minutes
away from indescribable happiness,
but also minutes away from potential
heartbreak.

James Milner sent the ball into the
Tottenham box from a corner, but
it was defended. The ball bounced
around outside of the area, and
Joël Matip passed the ball to Origi.
On his own in the box, Origi pulled
back his left foot and struck the ball.
To the fans, the shot looked as if it

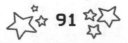

were traveling in slow motion. Trent
watched on outside of the box, rooted
to the ground, as the ball sailed past
Lloris and into the net. Trent sprinted
to congratulate his teammate as the
tension and pressure was lifted off
their shoulders.

The team held on for the final few
minutes. In the last seconds, fans
in the stadium, fans at home and
the players on the field could barely
believe what was about to happen.
The referee brought the whistle to
his lips and blew. There were shouts,
cheers and tears of joy. The pain of

the previous year's final was all but forgotten now.

Liverpool FC had won the Champions League.

BREAKING THE THIRTY-YEAR CURSE

Liverpool entered the 2019/2020 season overflowing with confidence. The Reds had been unable to stop Manchester City from winning back-to-back Premier League titles, but they had

won the Champions League title and earned the right, for a year at least, to be known as the best team in Europe.

But now the time for celebration was over. It was time to focus on the trophy that the club craved above everything else: the Premier League title. Could this be the year they prized the trophy from Manchester City's grip?

Liverpool triumphed on the first day of the season with a firm 4-1 win against Norwich. Trent started the season in fine form by providing an assist for an Origi header during the match. Liverpool then went on to beat

Southampton in their second match, Arsenal in their third and Burnley in their fourth.

Liverpool carried the momentum from their Champions League trophy win and went unbeaten in the league for twenty-seven matches. They were performing so well that many tipped them to achieve an "invincible" season—a league campaign where a team goes unbeaten throughout the entire season. Then, to the surprise of everyone, Liverpool came unstuck on their 28th matchday. A Watford side facing relegation achieved a shock 3-0

victory against Liverpool. However, the Reds bounced back with a win against Bournemouth and refused to allow this setback to define them.

While Liverpool remained in control on the field, matters off the field were threatening to derail their title hopes. Catching them and everyone else in the world off guard was the growing COVID-19 pandemic.

Instead of thousands of fans roaring the team on toward a Premier League triumph at Anfield, those fans, the players and the coaches were at home under lockdown to help stop

the spread of the virus. Fans started to ask questions on social media. Was it possible for the Premier League to continue? Should Liverpool be declared instant winners due to their lead? Or the most talked about and controversial question of all: should the season be scrapped altogether, potentially preventing Liverpool from winning the title that had escaped them for thirty years?

Many meetings were held between the soccer bosses, and as the dust began to settle on the initial chaos, a decision was made. Helped by the postponed Euro 2020 tournament, the league would continue into the summer, under strict protocols and in empty stadiums. The public could still look forward to televised soccer during this difficult time. Liverpool fans, having feared the worst, could breathe a sigh of relief. The Premier League campaign, barring any major setbacks, would be finished in full for the 2019/2020 season.

Liverpool continued their league dominance despite a three-month break, and match by match they came ever closer to wrapping up the title.

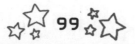

 But Liverpool's fate was not decided while they themselves were on the field. After Liverpool's 4-0 victory against Crystal Palace, there was no room for error for any of their rivals. If Manchester City failed to win in their tie against Chelsea, it would be mathematically impossible for Liverpool to lose the league.

On a cool spring evening, the Liverpool players, dressed in casual clothes instead of soccer gear, were watching the game on a TV in a hotel garden. They were scattered across the patio and grass, sitting in rattan chairs, watching in the knowledge that today could be the day. The thirty-year wait for a Premier League trophy for Liverpool FC could finally be coming to an end.

Trent was sitting by his friends, and teammates, not too far from the TV screen. He was glued to his seat, leaning forward, watching every kick. Chelsea's American forward, Christian Pulisic, had everyone at the hotel celebrating by firing Chelsea into the lead. However, Manchester City's De Bruyne levelled the score

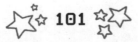

with an impressive long-range free kick. With just over ten minutes to play, Chelsea went on the attack and had an attempt cleared off the line by Fernandinho. However, following a closer look by VAR, it was deemed that he had prevented the goal crossing the line by flicking the ball away with his hand. Brandishing a red card for Fernandinho, the referee pointed to the spot and awarded a penalty to Chelsea.

Everyone at the hotel stood up and watched eagerly. Trent stared at the screen hoping to hear the sweet sound of the ball striking the net.

Chelsea's Brazilian forward Willian picked the ball up and placed it onto the spot. He ran up to it and fired it into the back of the net, sending everyone in the hotel garden into a frenzy. They were only minutes away from being crowned champions of the Premier League.

As the final seconds ticked away, the Liverpool team cheered, stamped their feet and banged their hands against the chairs like drums. The referee blew the whistle and the Liverpool players released a season's worth of tension.

Trent brought his hands to his head and tried to comprehend what he had achieved. He had played in every single game for the team in the Premier League season. He'd scored four goals and provided thirteen assists—a league record for a defender. He was an integral member of a Liverpool team that had finally broken their Premier League curse.

11
WHAT NOW?

Winning both the Premier League and Champions League at such a young age was a great achievement for Trent. The question for both him and Liverpool was where were they headed to next? Could they continue this run of form into the 2020/2021 season? Or would their rivals rise to

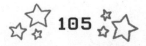

the challenge and knock them off their perch?

Their season got off on the right foot. Liverpool achieved three straight wins against Leeds United, Chelsea and Arsenal. However, in their fourth game came a result that shocked the entire league. Liverpool were defeated 7-2 by Aston Villa. In the previous season, Villa had been dangerously close to relegation. But now they had beaten the reigning champions! It showed that this season was not going to be like Liverpool's title-winning campaign,

and they needed to step up their game. After this blip, Liverpool went on a run of twelve games unbeaten. This included a 7-0 demolition of Crystal Palace at Selhurst Park.

During this winning run, Liverpool suffered a setback that would hinder their season. Their defensive leader, van Dijk, suffered a season-ending injury during a clash with local rivals Everton. The talented backline that Trent had

 played a key role in was changing shape, and not for the better.

One of the best defenses in the league soon became one of the worst. Disorganized and riddled with injuries, Liverpool lost eight out of twelve Premier League games during one of the worst periods in the club's history. They suffered defeats to Southampton, Burnley, Brighton, Manchester City, Leicester City, Everton, Chelsea and Fulham. This poor run of form led to Trent being left out of the England squad that Spring for World Cup 2022 qualifying matches. Worst of all, this was just before Euro 2020.

But Trent refused to give up.

He upped his game and so did the rest of the team. They went unbeaten during the last ten matches of the season. And when it mattered most, they finally broke into the top four in the league table. Despite a poor start to the season, Liverpool made sure they would be playing in next year's Champions League by finishing third in the table. Liverpool showed that they were not done yet and were 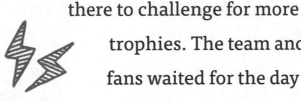 there to challenge for more trophies. The team and fans waited for the day

when their key players would be back from injury. Once the 2019/2020 title-winning players were back on the field together, they were sure to battle for the Premiership once again.

Although Trent had an up-and-down season, his impressive run of form at the end of the campaign created a problem for England manager Southgate. Despite England already having a heap of talent in the right back position, had Trent earned a return to the squad in time for Euro 2020?

12
ONE GAME AWAY

The moment the Premier League ended, everyone's focus switched to Euro 2020. Everyone had an opinion on who should be included in the final England squad, and Trent was one of the most talked about players.

England had a number of quality

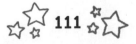

players who held the same right back position. Some believed that Trent's drop in form during the season meant that he didn't deserve a place. Others argued that with his natural talent and ability he should be one of the first names in the squad. Every sports newspaper, talk show and podcast discussed Trent. No matter what he did with his time, whether he switched on the TV, walked past a shop or scrolled through his phone, Trent struggled to escape the media frenzy that surrounded him.

Aware of the rumors, and in an effort to protect Trent, Southgate called him secretly three weeks before the squad announcement.

"Hi, coach," said Trent, picking up his phone. He wanted to play for England, and he hoped that he'd done enough to earn a spot in the team.

"I wouldn't usually call so early," said Southgate. "But the things we're reading in the papers are simply not true. We wanted to assure you that we have every faith in you."

A hopeful smile crept onto Trent's lips.

"Does that mean ...?" he asked.

"Yes, Trent. You've been picked. We're going to call up a larger squad of thirty-two. Then, after some training, we'll cut it down to the final twenty-six squad members. So get some rest, and then let's put a stop to all of this gossip!"

"Thanks, coach!"said Trent. He put the phone down and a wave of relief washed over him. Six players would eventually be cut, so he

 wasn't a certainty for the final squad. But at least he knew that he had a chance. And after the difficult season he'd played in, that meant everything to him.

Trent joined up with the squad and trained as hard as he could during every session. The days quickly flew by at St. George's Park, England's main training complex. Before he knew it, the squad announcement day had arrived. After all the speculation, hardships and rumors, Trent's fate was decided.

He'd been selected for the final twenty-six! Tears welled in his eyes as all of the emotion and frustration of

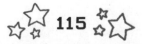

the difficult season came through. His hard work to get back to his best had paid off. Trent was going to Euro 2020!

Before the tournament began, England had two friendlies lined up to improve the players' match fitness and teamwork. The first match was a home tie against Austria. Trent had been named in the starting eleven, and with the weight of the squad decision now off his shoulders, he played with enthusiasm and the confidence of a world class player. His fierce forward runs troubled the Austrian defense during the match.

At one point, Harry Kane picked up the ball and made his way past a number of opposition players. Trent ran into the space on the right wing, and Kane found him with a neat long-range pass. Trent galloped forward with the ball and unleashed a venomous shot at the goal. The Austrian goalkeeper, Daniel Bachmann, leapt into the air, but he was saved as the ball flew over the crossbar. The home fans cheered on their team for such a fantastic effort. The substandard Trent was a thing of the past. This refreshed version was a

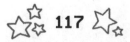

player that any opponent should fear.

Then, in the second half, in an instant, Trent's entire summer changed course.

In the final five minutes of the match, as England defended their one-goal lead, Trent made a clearance in his own half. Trent stretched with his weaker left foot to kick the ball. As he did, he let out a shout of pain. He brought his hand to his thigh and hobbled forward. His teammate Conor Coady came over to check if he was okay, but Trent knew that something was very wrong. He stared out into the stadium before signalling to the bench that he needed to be substituted.

Trent shuffled off the field and was helped to the locker room by the medical staff. Trent didn't have confirmation yet, but he knew that this wasn't just a minor knock. He feared the worst: that after all of the waiting and hoping he was going to miss the tournament due to an injury.

The next day, Trent was examined by the medical staff. He had an MRI scan to check for any soft tissue damage to his leg. Once the results

of the scan were in, the medical staff broke the news.

"It's not good is it?"asked Trent, holding his breath.

"It depends how you look at it,"said the doctor. "You've experienced a small tear to the muscle. The good news is that an injury like this only takes about four to six weeks to recover from. The bad news, I'm afraid, is that you will need to miss  the Euros. But with a strong recovery program, we'll have you back and running in no time."

Trent was devastated to miss the chance to represent his country at Euro 2020. He had made it so far, and performed so well, only to have it all undone by an unfortunate injury. He wanted nothing more than to wear the Three Lions shirt at the tournament. But he was also proud of his contribution, and knew just what this team could achieve together.

While the news was a great loss for Trent, it was a golden opportunity for another. Six players had been cut from the squad, but due to Trent's injury a place had now opened up. In Trent's place, young center-back Ben White was called up to the England squad.

Before leaving for his recovery, Trent went to see everyone and say his goodbyes.

"I'm gutted not to be playing," said Trent, leaning on his crutch as his teammates gathered around him. "But I'm excited to see what this team can achieve this summer."

"You've pushed us all in training," said Henderson, Trent's Liverpool and England teammate. "You've made a big impact on this squad that we'll carry into the tournament."

Trent smiled for the first time in a few days. "You boys better go on and win it then," he said.

England went on to have an incredible tournament. Although they were unable to win the trophy, they made it all the way to the final. It was the furthest an English team had ever gone in a European Championship. For the entire tournament, although not on the field, Trent was one of the team's biggest fans.

13
ROAD TO QATAR 2022

After Euro 2020 had wrapped up, most players switched off and took a break. But not Trent. He was away in Majorca, taking advantage of the warm weather to train and get back to full fitness. He was desperate to triumph over the injury that had derailed his summer. Trent set his sights on starting the 2021/2022 Premier League season in the best condition of his career.

Trent stepped out of the sliding doors of his Spanish villa and onto the patio. On the edge of the deck was a swimming pool stretching along the width of the garden. Beyond that was a stunning view of villas, green trees and terracotta-tiled roofs. As other players laid down to sunbathe, Trent turned on the treadmill. He stepped onto it and began to run. As his muscles

worked, his mind thought back to all of the things that had brought him to this point.

In his vision, Trent saw his home in West Derby with his family standing proudly outside. He started sprinting on the treadmill as he remembered long hours spent on the training fields in his hometown. His memory wandered through the academy complex and locker rooms where he had been coached and developed. Finally, he thought back to when he stepped out of the Anfield tunnel and onto the sacred

turf that he had dreamed of playing on throughout his entire life.

Trent had achieved his childhood dream. He was also a player for his hometown club and had led them to Champions League and Premier League success. He was also an England international player, and had only just missed out on a major tournament through injury.

With plenty of years left ahead of him in the game, Trent was determined to continue winning trophies, breaking records and

celebrating in front of thousands upon thousands of fans.

Trent increased the speed on his treadmill, sprinting as fast as he could. He wasn't going to let anything stop him from making the squad for Qatar 2022. For Trent, this was only the beginning.

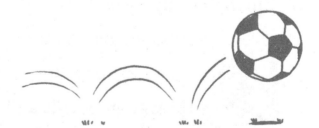